SARAH KORHNAK

Idea Craft

Discover the best small business idea for you!

First published by SBS Media LLC in 2016

First Edition

ISBN: 978-09995759-0-1

This book was professionally typeset on Reedsy.
Find out more at reedsy.com

Contents

Introduction

I get excited when people tell me they want to start their own small business. Nothing could be more thrilling than starting a business from scratch and earning extra income. Nothing beats the anticipation and enthusiasm of wondering just how far the business could go!

There are many reasons to start a business. Some people have always wanted to be an entrepreneur and have finally decided to go for it. Others start a business because they need to earn extra cash in addition to their nine-to-five job wages. Some people start a small business with the hope of quitting their day job at some point in the future. Still others are stay at home moms who want to stretch themselves in other ways during the day.

Whatever your reason for wanting to start a small business, I am excited for you! Creating a business will be one of the most challenging yet most rewarding things you ever do.

In my experience, individuals new to business form two camps. Those in the first camp know they want to start a business, but have no idea what kind of business to start. Those in the second camp of people pick the first business idea that pops into their head and start running with it, often to find, down the road, that their choice wasn't a great one.

This book is for both types of small business beginners. It is for those who want to earn additional income but have no idea where to start.

It's not enough to just pick any small business idea and go for it; you need to select the right idea for *you*! You are unique, and your business should match your passions and personality. How will you discover the right idea for you?

We will begin by brainstorming the topic of your business. The theme around which you will build your business is the topic.

Next, we will brainstorm about your personality and what you hope to achieve with your business. These elements play a significant role in the type of business that is a good fit for you. The business type is the form the business takes such as online store or blog.

After brainstorming, we will explore all the various types of businesses. Detailing all your possible choices will allow you to make the best business decision.

Finally, we'll bring it all together, and you'll craft the perfect small business idea for you. Your business idea is the marrying of the right business topic and the right business type. When the two come together, you have your ideal business idea!

Business Topic + Business Type = The Perfect Business Idea for You!

I have started many small businesses over the past decade. Some of those businesses have worked out well, and others have not. I've learned through trial and error the importance of being selective about the type of business to start, and about choosing a business that aligns with my personality and passions. What have I dabbled with? Craft shows, blogging, Etsy selling, podcasting, and selling on Amazon, to name a few! I have thoughtfully considered why some of these ideas worked better for me than others did. Throughout my business endeavors, I have heard the stories of hundreds of small business owners. I've compiled all of that information in this comprehensive and easy-to-understand book.

Once you have selected your perfect business, head over to my website, Small Business Sarah[1]. At Small Business Sarah I take the misery and mystery out of small business taxes and accounting. You know. The fun stuff! By quickly understanding and managing the financial side of your business from the beginning, you can then concentrate on running and growing your business. Sign up for my newsletter[2] to receive a free Small Business Startup Checklist to get you moving forward fast!

Learning from others is a great way to fast forward your business! To that end I created many Pinterest boards, each centered on a different type of small business. After you pick the right business for you, my Pinterest boards can immediately get you started with informative articles tailored to your business. You can find me on Pinterest at Small Biz Sarah[3].

Are you excited to get started? I am!

-Sarah

I

Exploring Business Topics and your Business Personality

The business topic is the theme around which your business is built.

When you have a clear picture of your business personality, you will be able to see clearly the types of business that will or will not be a good fit for you.

*Business Topic + Business Type = The Perfect Business Idea for **You**!*

1

Brainstorming the Topic

Every business is organized around one central topic. The Home Depot is built around the topic of Home Improvement. Starbucks rallies around the theme of coffee. Your favorite blog discusses a subject near and dear to you: saving money, parenting, humor, or decor. Your favorite Etsy shop may focus on antiques, textiles, or paper crafts. Big and small, every business centers its efforts on a central topic.

The first step in discovering *your* perfect business idea is to uncover the topic around which your business will flow. A brainstorming session is a perfect way to hash out potential topics for your business.

If you think you already know what your business topic will be, complete this brainstorming exercise anyway. A new idea may come to light, or you may discover a hidden topic you have not considered.

Set the Stage

To have a productive brainstorming session, set aside at least thirty minutes of distraction-free time. Turn off the TV and your phone. Make sure the kids are asleep or occupied. Alert your spouse that now is not the time to discuss the family calendar. Maybe a trip to your local coffee house will be your best bet for concentrated alone time.

Gather some materials on which to write your brainstorming responses. For tech lovers, open up a fresh Word document or Evernote note. For paper people, choose a fresh notebook, index cards, or sticky notes. Use whatever medium you enjoy most.

Slowly read through each of the following brainstorming questions and jot down the first response that pops into your head. Do not edit as you go. Simply record any thought you have related to that particular question. Write down what might seem silly, stupid, or insignificant. Write down responses from your professional life and your personal life. There are no wrong answers when you are brainstorming! You may have multiple answers for each question. Write them all down!

The Questions

What specific skills or specialized knowledge do you currently possess?

In what areas do you have specialized training?

What hobbies do you enjoy?

What are you passionate about?

What do you do well compared to others?

What do you find yourself thinking about all day long?

What problems do you have in your life?

What trials have you managed to come through?

What problems do your friends complain about?

What obstacles or fears have you overcome?

What would you like to learn more about?

In what areas would you like to grow or stretch yourself?

Have any books or blogs you've read lately sparked interesting ideas?

What products do you love to use around your home?

What are your strengths?

What are your weaknesses?

What service do you wish were available to you?

What services do friends remark that they would rather pay for than do themselves?

If you could get paid to make something for others, what would you create?

If you could get paid to provide a service for others, what would you do?

What do people appreciate your doing for them?

What do you enjoy doing in your free time?

What are the tasks or services that friends or associates ask you to help with?

If money were not a factor, what would you spend your life doing?

What websites and blogs do you read most often?

What do you enjoy doing so much that time just flies?

After brainstorming, begin to look for patterns in your responses. Do you see any recurring themes? What possible topics excite you the most?

Do not select your business topic yet! Reflect on your brainstorming responses over the course of the next few days or weeks as you continue to read this book.

Take time to talk with your spouse, close friends, and relatives. Ask them a few of these questions as they relate to you. What skills, knowledge, or talents do they appreciate most in you? Share with them your list of possible topics to gain their feedback. Sometimes, the people who love us see things we miss about ourselves. Ponder their advice and the results of your brainstorming sessions as you continue to explore potential business ideas.

2

Understanding Your Business Personality

You now have a long list of possible business topics after completing your first brainstorming session. For every business topic, there are many different types of businesses. By type of business, I mean the form that the business takes. For example, the topic of home improvement includes many different types of businesses such as retail stores, blogs, books, and home improvement services. Every business topic offers a range of business types.

Because each topic can be taken in many directions, it's imperative to carefully consider the type of business that is right for you. Your personality, strengths, weaknesses, time, and available capital all play a role in determining the type of business that is the ideal fit for you!

We are going to brainstorm once again to help you recognize how your personality affects the type of business that is ideal for you.

Set the stage one more time and grab your preferred brainstorming "paper."

The Questions

Do you enjoy personal interactions and working with others?

Do you prefer to work on your own?

Do you prefer center stage, or being in the background?

How much time do you have to devote to your venture?

Do you want full-time income or a side income?

What form of social media do you enjoy using the most?

How much money can you invest in starting your business?

Do you like to write?

Do you enjoy being on video?

Do you like to make things with your hands? Are you "crafty?"

Do you enjoy teaching and instructing others?

Do you always have things to say, or are you more the quiet type?

Do you consider yourself friendly and outgoing, or shy and reserved?

Are you comfortable sharing personal information on social

media?

Once again, consider talking with close friends and family about personality traits they notice most about you. Ponder your answers to these questions and the thoughts of loved ones, as we explore possible business types throughout the rest of this book.

II

Exploring Business Types

There are many ways to start a business. A small business can take many forms. In order to properly choose the type of business that is right for you, you need to have an understanding of all available possibilities.

*Business Topic + Business Type = The Perfect Business Idea for **You**!*

3

Product Sales

When you first decided to start a business, perhaps selling a product was your first idea. Selling products can be a great way to start a business, but there are many ways to pursue a business that sells products. There are two basic categories of products: products you've made yourself and products made by someone else. Keep these product categories in mind as you read through the descriptions of various product-based businesses. Either product type could be a business option for you in ways you have yet to consider.

Products can be sold for every business topic you can think of! Since there are so many ways to sell products, there are certainly ways to sell that will be a great fit for your personality. Product sales can have a couple drawbacks. The first is the capital to get started. Whether you use that capital to buy raw materials to make handmade items, or use the capital to purchase a stock of inventory, an initial investment will be required. The second drawback to product sales is the space requirement. You will need space to store your materials, finished products, inventory items, and shipping materials and supplies. The amount of space you need will vary depending on the product and method of selling you choose. These drawbacks may not be a problem for you but must be considered as you continue to investigate a business in product sales.

In Person Product Sales

Retail Storefront

There is something beguiling about the thought of having your very own store. The cute little store in my mind's eye has a dainty bell that jingles pleasantly each time a happy customer enters. And yes, the customers are always happy!

A physical store paints a lovely picture, but the start-up capital required to begin such a venture would be significant. Not only is rent a consideration but a significant amount of money would also be required for the initial purchase of inventory. If capital is available, and you have the ability to be at your shop many days a week, and the thought of daily interactions with customers is something you would enjoy, then a storefront could be an option for you. For most of us, it's not the easiest place to start.

Craft Shows

A simpler way to sell products in person is at craft shows. Every community across the country has a craft show or two. If your products sell well at craft shows, you can travel to larger shows in nearby towns, states, or across the country.

The primary advantage of selling at craft shows is the immediate feedback you receive from customers. As they browse your products, you'll hear their comments and questions, and in return, you can ask them questions about their preferences.

When you introduce new product lines, craft shows allow you to gauge immediate feedback on the new items and make adjustments quickly. By listening to your customers, you will learn how to get slow sellers moving, gain an understanding of how customers feel about your prices, and get customers' thoughts on new products they would be interested in.

Depending on the craft show, you may not need to have a handmade product. Some craft shows limit exhibits to handmade items, but others allow other types of products to be sold.

If you enjoy interacting with people and have the ability to work on Saturdays (the day most craft shows take place), then selling at craft shows may be a great business model for you.

Home Parties

Everyone is familiar with national home party companies such as Pampered Chef or Premier Jewelry, and aligning yourself with one of these companies may be a perfect fit for you. Home parties can also be a great strategy to use in selling your own products. The products you sell at home parties can be handmade or products that you buy in bulk at wholesale prices to resell. Angie Gordon of the Etsy shop Gathered and Sown[4] uses home parties to increase sales of her handmade purses at Christmas time. Angie invites a few friends who also make handmade products, and each seller invites friends to attend the home party. It is a great opportunity for friends to begin Christmas shopping while supporting small businesses, and it is a great way for the sellers of handmade items to get early Christmas sales and gain immediate customer feedback. Angie's home parties eventually became so successful that she began her own craft fair! A friend of mine, Christina, sells all-natural body products that she makes in her home. She uses home parties to spark interest in her new items. She puts a fun spin on her home parties by using the make-and-take format in which party guests select a product they want to make and then take it home with them. As party guests make their own all-natural products, Christina walks around explaining the health benefits of the products and educating us on the benefits of using essential oils. Party guests can also place orders for additional items at the party. The make-and-take format could be used with a variety of handmade products. The benefit of a make-and-take party is that guests are at ease, involved and informed, and don't feel as if they're receivers of a sales pitch. Just as the national brands do, you should, at the end of the party, encourage guests to host a make-and-take home party and offer the hostess free products in exchange for use of her home. Use the personal interaction with your customers to grow and adjust your products and offerings.

The major drawback of the in-person sales format is that you invest time in making or sourcing your products, and you invest a significant amount of time on the sales end as well. With the in-person model, you need to be present to sell your products. This may be good or bad depending on your personality and your available time.

Online Sales

The obvious advantage to online sales is that you can sell without being present at the time of sale. Online sales offer more flexibility as to when you work and allow you a buffer between yourself and the customer. The most difficult challenge with online sales is driving the customer base to view your products in your online shop and, hopefully, make a purchase. The technological aspect of selling online can be confusing and complicated, but by using an existing platform, many of the technological headaches can be eliminated.

Existing Platforms

Using an existing platform is an excellent way to begin selling online. Etsy is the obvious choice if you sell handmade products, vintage items, or craft supplies. If you sell used items or items you buy in bulk at wholesale prices, then eBay is a great choice. Amazon is a great place to sell used, new, or handmade!

The primary advantage to using an existing platform is that the platform helps to drive traffic your way. When customers search on Etsy, eBay, or Amazon they can find your products as one of their search results. The downside to the use of an existing platform is that you must abide by the host's rules and pay fees for the privilege of selling on the host's site. In addition you are competing with other sellers of the same or similar product and the competition for sales can be tough!

Etsy

I started my Etsy shop, The Amateur Naturalist[5], with my sister in the fall of 2012. Now I run the shop on my own. Etsy has been a great place for me to sell my handmade products and to slowly add supplies as well. Etsy makes it easy for sellers to get started and its platform is also easy to use. Etsy provides many features that make running the shop and shipping orders super simple. Seller fees on Etsy are very reasonable at only $.20 to list an item and 3.5 percent when an item sells. Etsy does restrict what items you can sell. Only handmade items, vintage items, or craft supplies are allowed. If your product does not fit into one of these categories, then you will need to investigate other platforms or options.

Etsy gives sellers flexibility in customizing their shop and setting their own policies. Customers can pay with PayPal or credit cards and the money is deposited into the seller's bank account weekly. Shipping is simple because sellers can create shipping rules for each product or let Etsy calculate the exact shipping fees for each customer. When sellers get an order they simply print the shipping label from Etsy and attach it to their package. In most areas, the United States Postal Service will pick-up packages for free! Such a deal! What service!

Another interesting possibility on Etsy is selling digital products. Many Etsy sellers do very well selling digital download items such as wall art printables, planners, checklists, invitations, or party supplies. When you sell a digital item, the customer simply receives an email from Etsy with the link to download their purchased item. No shipping required!

My favorite source for spot-on Etsy advice is Melissa Kaiserman from Makery Space[6]. She knows absolutely everything about Etsy!

Amazon

I recently began experimenting with selling on Amazon. I began with items I already had around the house that were like new and that I thought would have value on the Amazon marketplace. Amazon makes selling items that already exist on its platform super simple. Sign up for an Amazon seller account, find the item you have to sell on Amazon, click a little button on the product page that reads "Have one to sell?" and set your price - and you're ready to go.

Amazon lets you choose whether to ship the product yourself, or ship the item to an Amazon warehouse which will ship it for you. I am experimenting with both methods.

The advantage of selling on Amazon is the wide range of products you can sell. You can sell your own product by creating a new listing from scratch, find used, low-priced products to resell at a profit, or buy wholesale items to resell. You can sell items that range from brand new to very used. You can ship items or choose to have Amazon ship. The amazing flexibility Amazon provides combined with the global reach of Amazon's customer base, makes this an ideal platform for product sales.

The disadvantage with Amazon is that its fees are high and the competition is fierce! Fees range by product category and by shipping method, but prepared to pay up to 15 percent in fees. Don't be discouraged by the high fees, but plan for them when researching this option. Many people make a full-time living by selling on Amazon and many companies have increased their sales tremendously by offering their products for sale in the Amazon marketplace.

eBay

eBay is a well-known platform for selling almost anything! It's a great place to sell items that aren't a great fit for Etsy or Amazon. eBay has fewer restrictions on what you can sell and how you can sell it. You can also create your own eBay shop where customers can see all the items you have for sale on eBay.

Items such as used clothing and toys seem to do well on eBay. If you want customers to bid for your unusual antique or other items, eBay is the answer. Bidding for an item creates competition and an atmosphere of excitement that often results in customers paying more for an item than they might otherwise! Don't forget, your unique handmade items can also reach a market on eBay. Fees on eBay generally max out at 10 percent.

The major disadvantage of all the platforms we have just discussed is that you don't get to keep your customers' email addresses in order to build an email list of your own. In chapter 10, Business Essentials, I discuss further why an email list is so important for business growth.

Your Own Online Shop

If the well-known shopping platforms are not a great fit for your product or idea, creating your own online shop may be an option. With your own online shop you can completely control the look and feel of your shop, control what you sell, manage the fees to a reasonable level, and avoid competing against other sellers on the same website. Whether you manufacture a product, create handmade products, or resell wholesale items, your own unique online shop could be the option for you.

There are several ways of creating your own shop. One option is to completely customize your own website or hire someone to create a custom website from scratch. This option gives you the most control over your online store but is the most expensive and time consuming option.

If you already have a website or blog, many plug-ins are

available to help you create an online shop and shopping cart system. WooCommerce[7] is one of these.

If you don't have a website or blog, or want the ease of creating a professional-looking shop with many built-in features, then an online shop-creator website may be the answer. I am most familiar with Shopify[8], which does an excellent job of simplifying online shop creation. There are other vendors such as Big Commerce[9], Big Cartel[10], or Wix[11] that are also good options.

Whatever method you choose to create your very own online store, the individuality and customization aspect is clearly the major advantage. The disadvantage to setting up your own online store is that you must drive all the traffic to your store in order to make any sales. A big misconception among those new to online business is that if you build it, they will come --people, that is. This is quite untrue. If you create an online store, you will need to spend a significant amount of time on marketing and traffic-driving activities.

Subscription Box Business

A popular new type of business is the subscription box business. Customers sign up to receive a new box of goodies delivered to their door each month. This concept works well because it combines the excitement of a surprise gift and the fun of getting something in the mail. What's not to love? Sometimes, with a subscription box business, you buy in bulk and at a discount the items you will be including in that month's box. Other times, companies will send you items for free to be included in the subscription box as a form of advertising for their product. This second method of obtaining items for your boxes will be more feasible as you build a strong list of subscribers and a reputation as a desired subscription box brand.

Subscription box businesses can be created for any topic: fashion, pets, kids, or crafts, for example. A subscription box service can be catered to appeal to any group of people. Cratejoy[12] is a service you can use to help manage your subscription box business.

Wholesale

Many new entrepreneurs fail to consider wholesale activities as a possibility when they are starting a business or scheming their first idea. The world of wholesale can provide many opportunities for a start-up business.

Wholesale Your Own Products

Selling your own handmade products wholesale may be a perfect first step for your product idea. When selling a product wholesale, you sell it for about 50 percent of the suggested retail price to a larger company that buys many wholesale products to resell. One of the most important components of wholesale is pricing. Can you produce your products at a low per-item cost that will net good returns at a wholesale price? The advantage of selling your products wholesale is that most of the selling and advertising is done for you by the store purchasing your items. This leaves you free to concentrate on product creation.

As you sell wholesale to more and more stores, your sales volume can increase rapidly. The disadvantage is that you have less control over how your product is sold and marketed.

For the privilege of selling in volume to a store, you make less per item than if you had sold the item at retail yourself. When I talk about selling products wholesale, I don't mean selling products to retail giants such as Walmart or Target (although it would be awesome to get to that level some day!). I'm referring to selling products to local stores and boutiques that cater to customers who would love that particular product. If you produce handmade soaps, look to small spas that have all-natural products for sale. If you produce handmade baby items, contact baby boutiques. You get the idea! Imagine how quickly you could build your business by constantly adding new boutiques to sell your wonderful products!

Wholesale Buying and Reselling

Another way to work with wholesale products is to be on the retail side. You can purchase wholesale products from other manufacturers to resell. There are many manufacturers, who sell their products at wholesale prices to businesses of all types. To purchase from these manufacturers you usually need to submit a simple form with your business information, federal EIN number, and state sales tax number. Sometimes, these businesses demand large minimum orders, but not always. If the idea of being in the business of selling products is intriguing to you, but you don't have a product of your own, buying from wholesalers to resell could be a great start.

You can sell the products you purchase at a wholesale price in all the ways we already discussed: selling items at retail, including on platforms such as Amazon, at home parties, or on your own online store. Selling items you buy wholesale has the advantage of eliminating the need to create your own products.

The downside is that you are limited by what your wholesale dealers produce or don't produce. For example, maybe you found an item that you can buy and resell and that always makes a great profit. Your business could change drastically if the wholesaler raises the price or discontinues the product, things over which you don't have control.

I have had experience with wholesale both as a seller and as a buyer. As a seller I have sold my handmade items to boutiques and other retailers. As a buyer I purchase raw materials from wholesale companies, and use the raw materials to make my handmade products.

I personally have not had great success as a wholesale seller and have decided to concentrate on selling my items at retail through my Etsy shop.

However, buying my raw materials at wholesale and using them in my handmade products has been extremely helpful to my business. By buying materials at wholesale prices I am able to significantly reduce the cost to make each item, thereby increasing my profit on each item. Don't assume you can't buy wholesale just because you are a small company.

Niche Sites

Niche sites are a very interesting type of online business. I'm including them in product sales because you sell others people's products, without ever touching inventory! Sounds crazy, right?!

The idea of a niche site is to pick a topic with which you can rank well in Google search. To succeed with your niche site, you will need to have a firm understanding of search engine optimization (SEO). You build a website entirely around a specific topic and add content to help your website turn up in Google search for that topic. You dive deep into only one narrow topic to keep your website focused. Throughout your website you will be recommending and mentioning products related to your topic. When you link to these products, you will use your affiliate link, which nets you a certain percentage of each sale. Having enough traffic to generate sales is key with a niche site.

If you create your niche site correctly, it's a great opportunity to earn passive income. Passive income means you earn money when you're not actively working on the project. Once your site is populated with high-quality content centered around one narrow topic and related recommended products, you could be earning money while you sleep! People who succeed at developing a lucrative niche site often continue to create additional niche sites based on different topics, thus enhancing their portfolio of websites that earn passive income. This is not a quick-fix business idea. This idea will also require a lot of up-front time researching how to create effective niche sites . In addition, it takes time to fill out a niche site and generate enough traffic to produce income.

Sound intriguing? Pat Flynn[13] is an expert at niche site creation, online marketing, and driving traffic to a website. His site is a great place to get more information.

4

Service-Based Business

Launching a service-based business can move your entrepreneurial dreams forward. Today people value their time more than their money. They are happy to pay someone else to complete a job that they don't like doing, don't have time to tackle, or would struggle to complete.

There are a zillion possibilities for service-based businesses you can create. Every topic has the potential for a service-based business. In addition, because service-based businesses can be structured in many ways, they can be great for introverts, extroverts, people who need flexibility, and entrepreneurs with or without capital.

In order to create a truly phenomenal service-based business, you must be willing to think creatively. Think outside the traditional box of bookkeeper or dog walker. Dream up a brand-new service that you could offer to your community.

Professional Services

Accountants and lawyers are among the most likely professionals to have a service-based business. However, with a little creativity, there are many other professions that could lend themselves to a small business.

In the online space, there is a need for graphic designers, website creators, marketing experts, app creators, computer coding experts, customer service representatives, audio experts, and the need for more such services is growing rapidly. Many online businesses wisely farm out skills they lack to professionals who can do the job well.

Outside of the online space, many professionals have opportunities to start their own business. Expertise in computers, technology, organizing, photography, and interior decorating comes to mind. The TV show *Royal Pains* features the creation of a concierge medicine practice!

Several decades ago there was no such thing as a professional organizer, and now personal organization is a common service people are willing to pay for. How could you use your professional training creatively to meet the needs of people around you?

Other Skills

In addition to professional skills; abilities, talents, and hobbies can be the foundation of a service-based business. Outdoor services are blooming with grass cutting, gardening, landscaping, and landscape design as sought-after services. Indoors, skills in repair and maintenance, painting, baking, babysitting, catering, tutoring, event planning, and cleaning present potential business opportunities. And don't forget the pets! Pet walking, pet sitting, pet grooming, and pet pampering services are part of a growing business field catering to pet lovers.

Rental Businesses

If you have available capital, then starting a business with rental properties is a smart move. In general, real estate appreciates, and your rental income pays off the rental property mortgage!

For most of us, getting started with real estate is a bit beyond our immediate capabilities. However, other types of rental businesses can be started. Thinking about what larger companies are renting inspires ideas about scaling down and starting small with a similar concept. Large rental industries that come to mind are construction equipment, furniture, or even musical instruments that elementary school students rent when they begin taking lessons at school. Is there a specialized niche where you see a rental need?

Some interesting and real-life examples of rental businesses are in the fashion industry. There are companies that allow you to rent everyday items for your wardrobe, fancy dresses and purses for special events, and even designer children's clothing for your special family photo shoot.

Apply the rental service businesses model to creatively develop a new business idea around your topic!

Virtual Assistants

Virtual assisting has grown rapidly over the last few years. A virtual assistant works online to assist other business owners. You can work for multiple business owners, or just one.

Some virtual assistants specialize. Social media management is a fairly common specialization. Other virtual assistants are willing to undertake a variety of tasks. Tasks a virtual assistant might handle include email management, appointment scheduling, web design, book formatting, audio formatting, social media management, graphic design, blog post uploading, content editing, content creation, data entry, order fulfillment, customer service --and the list goes on! If you have skill in any of these areas, then starting a virtual assisting business may be a great way for you to immediately begin earning income.

You can find virtual assisting jobs by reaching out to Facebook groups, getting in touch with bloggers you follow, through referrals, or by word of mouth.

If finding work as a virtual assistant is proving difficult, you could start with a website such as Fiverr[14]. On Fiverr, you can post any job you are willing to do for $5. Don't be fooled by the low price. Many people have been able to earn full-time incomes on Fiverr. Whether or not you post your services on Fiverr long-term, it can be a great way to hone your craft, get experience working with clients, develop your resume, and possibly, acquire a more permanent position.

Virtual assisting presents many ways you can offer services to other professionals. Focus on your skill set and your specialty. There is someone who is willing to pay for your help!

Think creatively about the service-based businesses you could start. You may never have heard of an exotic pet sitting service that takes care of pets such as snakes, guinea pigs, or lizards, but that doesn't mean you can't start such a service. Use the brainstorming questions at the beginning of this book to identify services you or your friends wish were available. The key to success is identifying the precise target market that would pay for what you have to offer, even if it has never been done before!

Many people (myself included) love supporting small businesses rather than large corporations. What better way to leverage the desire for the personal touch than to create a service-based business?

A small business is able to rapidly adjust to the needs of clients. Take advantage of that ability! You started a cake baking business, but everyone really wants cupcakes. Adjust! You started walking ten dogs at one time, but your customers were willing to pay more for the individual attention of walking one dog at a time. Adjust! You started a lawn cutting business, but your customers started asking you for gardening and design advice. Adjust! Take advantage of the flexibility and agility that a small business has over a large corporation. Pay attention to your best clients, focus on them, and rapidly adjust based on their needs.

5

Writing

Writing is extremely versatile as a business type because it easily accommodates any business topic. In this business type section, we will explore several ways you can begin a writing business. The writing businesses we will discuss are of the do-it-yourself variety, as opposed to relying on a publishing house to traditionally publish your work.

Blogging

Blogging has become a trendy way to start a business. More and more people are jumping on board and earning money from their blogs. Don't hop into blogging, thinking it's a sure fire way to make a quick buck. Blogging is the same as every other business in that it takes work to be successful.

There are many positives to starting a blog. A blog can be done in your own time and on your own schedule. Blogging requires very little start-up capital. A blog can be created around any topic, and grow with you as your interests and knowledge expand. The potential income from blogging ranges considerably. Some bloggers earn only a small amount of money from their efforts while others generate a substantial income.

Blogging requires a considerable amount of upfront time before any monetary gain is realized. Most bloggers spend six months to a year working on their blog until they begin to see some cash flow from their efforts. Other bloggers will work at it for years and never become successful.

Blogger's earn money in a variety of ways. Advertising used to generate a lot of income for bloggers, but advertising income is on the decline and no longer produces a significant income. Recommending other companies' products or services, called affiliate advertising, is a popular way to generate income. By recommending products or services through special links, you earn a portion of the sale price when people purchase. The most lucrative way bloggers earn income is by creating their own products or services. Many bloggers start by recommending other people's products and then slowly begin creating and selling their own products and services. Those products could be eBooks, courses, printables, coaching, and more.

A big misconception among non-bloggers is that it's a great fit for introverts. You can sit behind your computer and type away and not meet people face to face. However, the best bloggers gain huge followings by constantly interacting with their audience. They share details of their personal lives and have a big presence on social media.

How do bloggers gain readers and followers? Google search traffic is one way in which a blog post can be found by a reader, but the main traffic driver for blogs is social media. If you are not a fan of social media, you may want to consider a different business type!

For great blogging advice, I recommend my brother Donnie

and sister-in-law Abby who make a full-time income from blogging. You can find their blogging advice on their website Building A Framework[15].

eBooks

An eBook is a digital book. An eBook can be sold on your own website in electronic format or on a major retail website such as Amazon.

Writing eBooks has many of the same pros and cons as blogging. Writing can be done in your own time and on your own schedule with minimal costs for writing and publishing.

However, writing an eBook requires a significant time investment before you see a potential paycheck. Writing anything and uploading it to Amazon will not net you thousands of dollars. The most successful self-published authors produce quality books and spend a significant amount of time marketing their books.

As bloggers do, the most successful eBook writers engage with their audience through a website and social media. Perhaps, hermit writers still exist, but most have mastered the art of being social online.

What I love about eBooks is that you can try your hand at writing on a wide variety of nonfiction topics, or if you have always envisioned yourself writing a superb novel, give fiction a try! It is fairly easy to get your book on Amazon. You can also turn your eBook into a paperback book with print-on-demand services such as Create Space[16], or make an audiobook through services such as ACX[17].

My favorite resource for creating a successful business based on self-published eBooks is Authority.pub[18]. In addition, you might consider joining a writing association for support in your writing journey.

Freelance Writer

Freelance writers get paid to write for other people. You can write for blogs, magazines, newsletters, brochures, ads, and so on. You can write promotional copy or ghostwrite.

The advantage of freelance writing over blogging or creating eBooks is the guaranteed paycheck. If you land a freelance gig and complete the job, you can expect to get paid. With blogging or writing your own eBook, you may write until you are blue in the face (or fingers!) and not see a dime.

Another plus is location independence. If you have always wanted to travel, creating a business that only requires a laptop and WiFi is perfect! You can complete your assignments from anywhere in the world!

One disadvantage to freelance writing is that you are working on another's timetable. If you agree to a deadline, you must meet it. If you tend to struggle with deadlines or project completion, this aspect may deter you from freelance writing as a business.

If writing books or a blog is at the top of your list of dreams, but you're nervous about waiting for the money to start rolling in, consider adding freelance writing as a side gig. Not only will you be honing your writing skills but you will also be earning money at the same time.

My favorite resources for learning how to rock it as a freelance writer are The Write Life[19] and Elna Cain[20].

6

Speaking

Do you harbor a secret dream of being a key-note speaker at a huge conference? Maybe you love the energy you get from talking with groups of people and sharing what you know. If your expansive personality needs a stage, then creating a business around speaking may be a great fit for you. Speaking can be a great fit for extroverts and spotlight seekers!

Well-known speakers don't start out on the big stage, they start small, slowly developing their skill and reputation for quality content. As they continue to refine their craft, they eventually work their way up to huge conferences, the main stage, and the paycheck to match. Let's talk about different ways you can get started on your small business based on speaking.

Specialty Groups

Regardless of your business topic, there are specialty groups that want to hear from you. These specialty groups are large and small and meet in a variety of places.

Women love any excuse to get together, and various women's

groups are always on the lookout for speakers. One example that comes to mind is church women's groups. My church has a Mothers of Preschoolers (MOPS) group that has hosted a variety of speakers throughout the years. A wide array of topics have been presented by these speakers including parenting, gardening, budgeting, meal planning, organizing, exercise, nutrition, mental health, safety, and financial planning. Our speakers have not only included women from our own group but also outside experts, both male and female. MOPS is certainly not the only type of group around, so explore your own community for groups you can contact.

Libraries are another great place to get started as a speaker. My library frequently hosts speakers on a variety of topics including travel, financial planning, writing, and cooking. In addition, the library newsletter frequently mentions that the library is looking for new speakers to come and address patrons on any variety of topics. The libraries within a short distance of your home could provide many opportunities for speaking engagements.

Your local community may have other groups that meet regularly. Gardening clubs, book clubs, writing groups, and outdoor enthusiasts can be found in many communities, and they might welcome a presentation on a topic important to them.

Many businesses may need a speaker for their work force. Every profession welcomes training in their particular field of expertise, and many are required to obtain a certain amount of continuing professional education training. Other types of professional training may also appeal to various businesses. For example, during my time working for a public accounting firm, we had speakers on various non-accounting topics such as professional dress code, public speaking, and professional client interaction. These presentations were given by a paid speaker outside the accounting profession.

Other businesses also bring in speakers to train or teach their workforce. Some hospitals host lunch time speakers for their nursing staff on a variety of topics. Time management experts are hired to teach professionals how to manage their work hours. Organizing experts teach professionals how to keep their paperwork and computer files in order. Communications experts teach employees at all levels how to be more professional in communications with customers. There are many opportunities for teaching and training various types of work forces, and because the speakers are paid by the company, they are often paid well for their time.

Start small to gain valuable experience speaking, presenting, and interacting with your audience. Starting small allows you to have the opportunity to gauge the reaction of your audience, and gain valuable feedback about your presentation. As you climb the speaking ladder, conferences might be your next venue. Conferences need fresh voices to meet the needs of their audience. After you gain experience at smaller events, you'll be ready to approach these conferences with confidence and a resume.

Extroverts are energized by their interactions with people. If you thrive on that type of energy, then becoming a speaker may be a great fit for you. The downside of public speaking is that it is location and time specific, lacking in flexibility. Earning income as a speaker can be tough and tedious. Many small groups do not pay their speakers, or they pay very little. Many famous speakers who now command audiences of thousands talk about their early days of public speaking when an audience of three people might be all they could expect. As with anything rewarding, if you are willing to put in the effort, the results can be amazing. Imagine being flown all over the world to give key-note speeches at top events and conferences! If that sounds like the ideal lifestyle for you, don't be afraid to pursue it wholeheartedly!

For practical advice on public speaking and practical application head to Toastmasters[21].

Podcast

What is a podcast? It's an audio program that can be listened to online or from a smart phone. Podcasts come in many formats. They can be an audio blog, a single person discussing a specific topic, interviews and group conversations, or they can tell a story.

A podcast can be started by anyone on any topic. You can start one on your own or with a team. Producing a podcast helps you improve your skills as a speaker. As you listen to and edit your own podcast you begin to notice all your speaking quirks, and once revealed, you can work to eliminate them. Podcasting helps you to be mindful of how you speak and the words you use while recording, speaking to a group, and in conversation. It's a great way to improve your public speaking skills.

Podcasting has a few technical start-up hurdles to overcome, but once you learn the process of producing your own podcast it becomes fairly straightforward and simple. As a former podcaster, I can assure you that it is possible for non-techie people to start and produce their own podcast.

Although a podcast can be perfect for an extrovert personality, it also works well for introverts. I am definitely an introvert but absolutely loved creating podcasts with my sister. I believe podcasting works well for introverts because they can talk into their computer while enjoying the seclusion of their own home. Although what they record will eventually be heard by potentially thousands, when they are recording they are their only audience!

Podcasting is usually combined with a website. Because a podcast is purely audio and hosted by other applications (e.g. iTunes, Stitcher), you need your own "home" where listeners can learn more about you, read show notes, and sign up for your email list.

As a podcaster, you can make money when you begin to add sponsors to your podcast. Advertisers pay for you to talk about their product or service or read an ad during your podcast. The more downloads you get per podcast, the higher the price you can charge for ads.

Another way to earn money with a podcast is by selling your own products, such as a book or course. The product should be closely related to the topic of your podcast. Many listeners who would otherwise not have found you online may find you from your podcast. This provides additional opportunities for you to sell your product to a whole new audience.

Podcasting can be done anywhere. If you have a solo show, you can record your podcast at anytime. If you choose an interview format, you will need to record your interviews at a time that is convenient for your interviewee, limiting your flexibility. You will need to consider this potential flexibility issue as it relates to your circumstances.

My favorite resource for podcasting is Pat Flynn. He has a comprehensive and free tutorial on getting started with podcasting on his website Smart Passive Income[22].

7

Teaching

There is always something you know more about than someone else. You may only have a moderate knowledge of gardening, but a gardening novice knows absolutely nothing. You can teach what you know to someone else who is just starting out. You don't need to be a world-class expert to teach; you only need to know more than your pupil!

Teaching can be great for the introvert or extrovert, depending on the chosen teaching method. It also requires very little capital to get started.

In-Person Teaching

Traditionally, teaching has been done in person. There are still many opportunities for this method of teaching.

Your local community college may be a great place to start. Community colleges offer a variety of community education classes on topics such as gardening, computers, cooking, painting, pottery, starting a business, writing, and more. Most community colleges accept proposals from local residents who have suggested a class they would like to teach.

Another teaching option is to create your own class. Maybe several of your friends or acquaintances have asked you questions about your specific area of expertise. You could begin holding informal classes in your home or local coffee shop. Angie Gordon of the Etsy shop Gathered and Sown[23] was getting a lot of questions from people she met in local Facebook groups about how they could start their own Etsy shops. Angie asked her favorite coffee shop if she could use its meeting room to teach a class. She charged a nominal fee for each participant and was able to offer specific and tailored advice to each person in her class. Her students spread the word, and Angie continued to hold classes, teaching others how to develop and manage successful shops on Etsy.

Teaching a class in person can be a great way to make connections and build relationships with people interested in your topic. In addition, teaching a small group allows you to tailor your class to the specific needs of your students and to offer personalized advice.

Small group settings that you might want to consider are retirement homes and independent living facilities. Many such facilities welcome classes on a variety of topics.

Teaching one-on-one in your home is another way to teach others. I grew up taking piano lessons from a woman, in her home. In-home lessons can be given for any instrument you have mastered.

Tutoring is another popular way to give in-home instruction. Former teachers can help struggling students after school.

Most of us think personal trainers are relegated to a gym, but in-home services may be just what a self-conscious client prefers, or the convenience of such a service may be what a busy professional is looking for.

If you think outside the box, you'll find that many skills can be taught in your home or in a client's home. Private knitting lessons, sewing lessons, yoga lessons, photography lessons, computer lessons, swimming lessons, or cooking lessons, can all be taught from home.

Online

Teaching online is another great way to share your expertise with others. By taking your teaching online, you can reach a larger audience of interested students. There are a couple ways to teach online. One is to provide personal attention live to students through a program such as Skype. The other way is to create an online course, in which students can learn their chosen subject through guided written information and prerecorded videos.

Skype

Skype[24] is a program that allows you to have free video phone calls with people all over the world. With Skype, you participate in a real-time video chat, thus it is the perfect tech savvy way to teach one-on-one or in small groups. Although Skype is a modern way to communicate with others, the program is simple to operate. Using Skype, you could give instrument lessons, crochet lessons, language lessons, or lead a yoga session. I also know of at least one professional organizer who helps clients organize their homes through Skype sessions! That is certainly a creative way to teach using technology!

If you choose to teach using Skype, you will need a way to advertise your services and showcase your expertise. This would most likely be done through a website of your own. Skype is merely the tool that will allow you to video chat with your students once they find you. It is not a means for advertising your services to prospective clients. Your website should clearly explain your background and expertise in your field and have a way for prospective clients to contact you. In addition, it would be wise to include helpful articles on your topic to demonstrate your knowledge to prospective students.

Platforms for Online Courses

Online courses are growing rapidly, and so are the platforms that host courses. Online courses offer students the opportunity for in-depth learning on a chosen topic. Many courses are self-guided: students who sign up for the course can go through the material at their own pace. Sometimes participants work through course material in a group so that the topic can be discussed with the course instructor at one time. Course materials are presented as a series of written instructions, helpful printables and checklists, and prerecorded video presentations. There are several platforms that can aid in course creation.

Teachable[25] helps guide you in easily creating and customizing your own online courses. You pay a small transaction fee or a monthly fee to host the course on the Teachable website. The upside to Teachable is its low cost, the ability to brand your course to your business, and your ownership of all student email addresses. The downside is that you must market your own course and drive all the traffic to your Teachable course. The site does not market courses for you. Any course topic is up for grabs on Teachable.

Udemy[26] is very similar to Teachable in that it allows you to easily create your own online course. Udemy's major difference lies in its control over the course and the marketing. Udemy has much more control over the course you create and can put your course on sale when it deems it advantageous to do so. In exchange for your giving up some control of your course, Udemy actively markets the courses available on its website. You can always drive traffic yourself, but you will also have traffic generated from Udemy's marketing efforts. Many course topics can be taught on Udemy.

Skillshare[27] focuses on smaller, bite-size videos to help people learn a new skill. Skillshare's system is a little different from the others we've discussed. Skillshare is a membership site. Members pay a small monthly fee and are able to watch as many videos as they like. How do teachers get paid? Every time one of your videos is viewed, you receive a small payment. In addition, when teachers refer people to Skillshare and they sign up for a premium membership, those teachers will receive a payment. As with Udemy, you are not alone when it comes to marketing your video. Customers can browse for courses including yours, plus Skillshare does some marketing of its own.

Consulting

A popular and lucrative way to teach others is through consulting. Consulting requires a high level of expertise. Once you have established yourself as an expert on a topic, you can consult on that topic for a high rate of pay. You can consult in person, over the phone, through email, or through Skype.

Another interesting and new way to consult is through a

website such as Clarity[28]. On Clarity you set a per-minute rate for your expertise on a chosen topic. Customers pay to speak to you over the phone and answer their questions. You get paid your rate for the amount of time you spend with them. Pretty cool!

8

Video

The number of people who want to consume information via video is on the rise and new platforms and apps appear daily to take advantage of this growing trend. YouTube, the largest source of online videos, reports that it has over one billion users who watch hundreds of millions of hours of videos everyday![29]

Extroverts and the tech savvy among us are not the only ones who can benefit from the growing trend of video. Introverts can create videos that don't necessarily showcase their lovely face!

Many people who specialize in online video have splurged on expensive equipment, but often, your basic camera, laptop video cam, or inexpensive software is all you need to get started. And have no fear non-tech savvy individuals. Most user interfaces for online video make uploading or recording video a piece of cake!

YouTube

YouTube[30] is the obvious platform that comes to mind when you think of online video. YouTube makes creating your own video channel and uploading your videos super simple. Its huge user base allows your video to be found.

Video can take many forms. Many YouTubers take the approach of filming themselves discussing a certain subject, demonstrating a product, playing a video game, or recording a video diary.

For the non-performers, screen capture videos, videos of nature, or videos of others may be a compatible fit. With screen capture videos, you use software to record exactly what you are doing on your computer screen. This is perfect for computer game videos, slide show presentations, or to demonstrate expertise in a technical field on your computer.

The possibilities are endless when it comes to video topics, including animals, technology, pregnancy, toys, video games, wood working, software, instruction, humor, babies, exercise --and the list goes on! A YouTube channel can be created around any topic!

YouTubers make money from the ads they allow to be placed on their YouTube channel videos. Every time a viewer watches the ad placed on your YouTube video, you earn a small commission. It is very easy to set up ads on your channel, but it may be a challenge to get enough people to watch your videos to generate income from the ads! Income rates vary, but in general, you earn a few dollars for every 1,000 video views.

You don't have to rely on ad revenue to make money with YouTube. Some YouTubers use the power of video to sell products they have created or they use the video as an extension of their blog.

Other YouTubers make money by reviewing products. If you have enough subscribers, companies that want to get their product noticed will send you their product and often pay a small fee for you to perform a demonstration of the product on your YouTube channel. Famebit[31] is a website that helps YouTube creators get connected with brands for paid opportunities.

My favorite resource for information on video creation is Meredith of Vid Pro Mom[32].

Facebook Live

Facebook Live is relatively new and therefore packed with exciting potential. Facebook Live allows you to record and post live videos directly to your Facebook page. Your Facebook followers are notified when you go live, creating an instant audience. Once your live session is over, the recorded video stays on your page.

Facebook really wants Live to become a popular feature, so the word on the street is that preference is given to Facebook Live posts over other types of posts. This means that Facebook is showing Facebook Live posts to more of your followers than it would a regular Facebook post. In addition, Facebook will share your Live post with more of your followers than a similar video you post to your page from YouTube. Using Facebook's in-house tools and pet projects boosts your visibility to your followers.

The ways in which you could use Facebook Live are many. Whether talking about a topic, filming a demonstration, holding a Q&A, making a big announcement, or selling a product, using video can be a powerful and effective way to spread your message.

III

Craft Your Business Idea

*After exploring possible business topics and
discovering all the many business types, it's time to
craft your perfect business idea.*

*Business Topic + Business Type = The Perfect Business
Idea for You!*

9

Craft the Perfect Business for You!

When you first began reading this book, did you have any idea how many different ways you could turn your topic into a business idea? Mind boggling!

We started by brainstorming various topics around which your business could center. Hopefully, a few of those thoughts have developed as great possibilities.

Next, we brainstormed about your personality and life goals to help us filter through the types of businesses that would be best for your personality. Choosing the right type of business for your unique personality and season of life makes a huge difference to the ultimate success of your business.

Finally, we explored all the various types of businesses available to give you a broad picture of possibilities.

Now comes the fun part! It's time to combine the topic of your business with the type of business best suited to you. When the two combine, you have discovered your ideal business.

To help you combine your business topic with a business type let's talk through some examples that will, hopefully, get your mind crafting up your ideal business idea.

Examples

Outgoing mother of three with lots of energy but little time. Topic: Gardening.

A mother of three, might find it tricky to fit an in-person type business into her schedule. It's tough to bring three young kids anywhere! In-person service-based businesses, including in-person teaching and in-person speaking would be quickly eliminated.

Writing is a possibility, but this mother is outgoing so something a little less isolated might be more in tune with her personality.

A gardening blog is a possibility. Combining the gardening blog and activities with her children would be a unique twist, allowing her to do gardening activities with her children while simultaneously accomplishing projects for her blog.

My favorite idea for this mom, though, is YouTube videos! While the kids are napping or while Dad is home on the weekend, this woman can set up her camera in the yard and film videos of herself explaining some aspect of gardening or yard maintenance. A young and vivacious Martha Stewart! Her YouTube channel could focus on realistic advice and projects perfect for other young moms like her who enjoy being outdoors. These YouTube videos may, ultimately, lead to a blog, or maybe even an online course that teaches specialized gardening techniques.

Quiet single with a flexible regular work schedule. Topic: Animals

For an animal lover who enjoys spending time with furry creatures more than human creatures, a service-based business working with animals would be a great fit. This woman will, of course, have some interaction with the humans who own the animals she works with, but much of her time will be spent with the animals themselves. A dog walking service comes to mind, but other types of pet sitting and pet care would be a good fit as well. If she is a horse lover she could board and care for the horses of others as well as her own. If she loves small pets, a pet sitting service might be nice. If she is already an expert groomer, she could begin a grooming service. If she starts small and pays attention to her customers' wants and needs, she can slowly begin to add services or products that she knows her customers will pay for.

Extrovert newlywed with free weekends. Topic: Handmade Purses

The outgoing woman working a traditional nine-to-five job can start a side business working in the evenings and on weekends. In this example, I chose the topic of handmade purses, but any handmade product could fit in this scenario.

When launching a new venture, getting immediate feedback from customers and prospective customers is very important. It might be tempting for this woman to buy large quantities of inventory and begin mass producing a product she thinks everyone will love, only to discover that customers are looking for something a little different. In the beginning stages of a handmade business, it can be a great idea to make a few different types of several products, and sell them at a craft fair. The craft fair will give her immediate feedback on the products customers like and don't like. She can ask customers questions about features they would like to see added, patterns or colors they like, and price point preferences. With an outgoing personality, craft fairs can be so much fun! (And let's not forget that craft fair food is so delicious!)

As her business begins to grow, and she hones her products, she can begin to sell some of her products online and continue to broaden her client base.

She can also teach local classes to provide additional revenue streams during months when she is not otherwise engaged with craft shows.

Talkative woman who loves to keep up with the trends. Topic: Time Management

For the woman with the gift of gab, a podcast is the way to go! Podcasting is a trending form of information consumption. The popularity of smart phones has enabled people to listen to podcasts everywhere!

Time management is always a hot topic, and a podcast is the perfect medium for communicating time management tips and skills. Consumers of the podcast can listen to great time management advice while they fold laundry, do the dishes, or drive to work.

This woman should not be intimidated by the idea of starting a podcast. There are many free online tutorials on how to get started. As the podcast begins to grow, adding sponsors will help her earn revenue from her hard work. Creating an online presence or a blog component to her podcast is a great idea and can be a source of additional revenue streams. Course or product creation is also a natural next step for a podcast.

Introvert workaholic who loves getting up early. Topic: Romance.

Many writers are at their best in the morning. For the woman who loves those early morning hours and isn't afraid of hard work, trying her hand at writing a novel may be perfect. Incidentally, romance is always a top selling niche. So when her first romance novel is complete, she could have an audience of prolific readers to sell her book to.

Fun loving gal with lots of style and an old house. Topic: DIY.

DIY is hot, but for the fun-loving gal whose house is not, a DIY blog may be a good fit! She can earn money by spiffing up her own house and documenting her projects on a blog. Who doesn't love a good DIY tutorial on how to create awesome knock-offs, giving life to old furniture, or completely re-hauling a kitchen? DIY is huge and here to stay, so for the woman with more DIY ideas than she knows what to do with, blogging about her projects to supplement her income is a perfect combo.

Blogging provides opportunities to branch out into product creation, course creation, and video creation to help expand revenue sources. Speaking engagements, writing requests, or teaching opportunities are all avenues for blog and income expansion. With a platform that showcases the DIY gal's awesome talents, additional opportunities will present themselves.

Shopaholic who can spot a good deal. Topic: Beauty and Fashion

With an eye for fashion and a knowledge of all the latest beauty techniques, a woman with this skill set could soar with product sales.

Creating her own trend worthy product could be one place to start. She could make some sketches, hire a seamstress, and launch her product-based business online or in-person.

Making her own products is not her only option. Buying and reselling products may really scratch her itch to shop. Designer label brands often find their way into thrift stores, creating an opportunity for our shopaholic to resell those items on eBay or on her own website. (I was recently in a thrift store where the woman in front of me in line found a pair of $150 jeans for $5!) Another option is scouring retail stores for expensive cosmetics or fashion merchandise on clearance, thus creating an opportunity to resell those items on Amazon at a profit. If our shopaholic has a very specific target market in mind for her fashion style, buying wholesale and creating her own unique online shop could be the perfect fit (no pun intended!). Wholesale fashion can be found at trade shows around the country or from overseas vendors.

I hope these examples have opened your eyes to all the different ways a business can be born. Go grab your brainstorm pages and get ready to craft your perfect business!

Your Perfect Business

We have gone through all the steps! We have brainstormed possible topics for your business. We have brainstormed some personal components that could contribute to what type of business you choose. Finally, we have talked about all the different types of businesses to start. Now it's time to craft your perfect business idea!

Hopefully, as you read this book, some great ideas have

popped into your head. Take out your topic brainstorming page. What topic cropped up multiple times on your brainstorming page? What topic gets you really excited? What topic kept coming to mind as you read through all of the different types of businesses? Chances are one topic has really come to forefront throughout this book. Choose that topic to center your business on.

Now pull out your business type brainstorming page. As you read through the book which business types seemed to resonate most with your personality traits? What about your time and available capital? Did one type of business really get you excited? Did a certain type of business spark a lot of ideas for growth? What type of business are you itching to try? Choose that one!

Combine your topic with your business type and you are ready to go! You have just crafted the perfect business idea for you! Don't delay getting started. There is never a perfect time to begin a business. Talk with your significant others and get them on board with your plans. Begin to research and learn as much as you can about your chosen topic and type of business.

10

Business Essentials

No matter what form your business takes, there are a few business essentials that will help your business succeed.

Collect Email Addresses!

No matter what type of business you start you must collect email addresses and create an email list. Why is this so important? Your email list will contain the email addresses of people who love what you are doing. They love your product or service, and they welcome articles, info, and updates from you. These people want to read your next blog post, sign up for your services, or buy your products. They want to know where you are speaking and the title of your new book. These are your fans, your people. Your email list is your golden ticket to business success, and you own that list. You may have thousands of Facebook likes or Pinterest followers, but when social media algorithms change (and they always do), you'll end up being unable to reach many of those people who like and follow you. Your own email list gives you ownership and permission to enter inboxes. Algorithms may change, but those email subscribers are yours.

There are many email services available that make creating an email list, and sending emails simple. Some of the top service providers are MailChimp[33], AWeber[34], ConvertKit[35], and MadMimi[36]. Each has their own unique features and price points, so take a look at each to find the right one for you.

When I say that every business needs an email list, I promise you I mean absolutely every business. The dog walker should periodically email clients with new services added and a funny dog YouTube video. The craft show seller should be collecting email addresses at every show to let her customers know what shows she will be participating in next and new products she has created. The speaker should have a sign up sheet at every speaking event, and should be emailing her fans to notify them of future events or relevant articles. The writer should have a list and let fans know when her new book is coming out.

Is collecting email addresses always as easy as setting out a sign up sheet or putting a sign up form on your website? No. You must give people a reason to sign up for your email list. You need inducements. Online businesses can entice people to sign up with various digital freebies such as checklists, pretty printables, or entire chapters of books. In-person business owners can entice sign-ups with prizes, free merchandise, or coupon codes. The idea is to sweeten the deal to encourage and entice people to sign up and give you their email address.

Once you have their email address, treat these people well! They may continue to support your business for years to come. Don't spam them, don't sell their email addresses, and don't pester them with never ending sales pitches! Give to them generously and they will give back to you.

Have a Professional Online Presence

An online business has an online presence, but make sure it looks professional and is user friendly. The first impression your online site makes is important. If I land on a website that looks old fashioned and out dated, I subconsciously call into question the authority and reliability of the website, regardless of the subject matter.

For a person-to-person business, I would highly recommend adding an online component as your business grows and matures. A business Facebook page is one type of online presence, but keep in mind that not every person uses Facebook. A simple yet professional website is the preferred way to showcase your business online. When I am searching for local service providers, the first step I take is a Google search. Begin your elite dog-walking business through customer referrals, but as business begins to pick up, add a website where potential customers can learn more about you and your services. Include your prices and testimonials from happy customers.

Speakers should have a professional webpage with a resume and information about the topics on which they speak. The website should also provide a way for interested parties to contact the speaker. Videos of past speaking engagements, uploaded to the website, are a great way to demonstrate speaking skills to prospective clients.

An author should have a platform, a place where fans can connect with the author and her topic, where occasional blog post can be published, and certainly where readers can find a list of all the author's books.

Business Cards

Business cards may not be the tool they once were, but they still serve an important purpose. One question often asked during casual conversation at social gatherings is, "What do you do?" A quick explanation of your business and a business card in their hand is a simple and unobtrusive way to try to expand your client base. Connecting with people and referrals is still a powerful way to grow a business.

Social Media

Social media has emerged as an effective tool for generating business. Whether you use social media on a personal level or not, having a social media presence for your business will help you to expand and grow. It can be alarming to think about developing a presence on all the top channels such as Facebook, Pinterest, Twitter, LinkedIn, and Instagram. Rather than giving in to overwhelm or being frozen into inactivity, select one type of social media to embrace in the beginning and start there. There is a lot to learn about each social media platform and its unique strategies for success. By focusing on one at a time, you will gain confidence while still making progress. With social media, you don't necessarily have to do everything (at least not right away), but you do need to do something. A comprehensive resource for social media best practices is Social Media Examiner[37].

11

Expanding your Business

Combining Types and Building as you Go

We have discussed so many types of businesses so far, has your brain begun to churn with possibilities? I know mine has even as I write this book! So far, we have talked about single types of businesses, but to be fair, many businesses have multiple components to them.

For example, an author may begin her business as a writer, but when her books become popular, she could start to offer courses or seek opportunities for speaking engagements.

A blogger may discover an awesome product her audience would love, and open an online shop.

Someone who loves to teach, and begins by teaching locally, may soon branch out and begin teaching online, creating courses, or making YouTube videos about her subject matter.

The right combination of business types or components can expand a business and create sales funnels that grow other areas of a business as well. A sales funnel, what is that?

A sales funnel occurs when customers are offered a certain product designed to funnel them into other products or services.

For instance, the author of a book series may offer the first book in the series for free in order to entice readers into buying the other books in the series. A course creator may offer an introductory course in order to encourage sales of her advanced course. A product creator may do speaking engagements and demonstrations for free to drum up sales of her new product.

Many business types can be combined in symbiotic ways to reach a wider market and ultimately bring in more revenue. Consider all possibilities when determining your best possible business idea.

You don't need to implement business combinations from day one of your business start-up. Start with one business type but constantly think about ways in which you could expand your business, create sales funnels, or reach a larger audience.

Dream Big, but Avoid Overwhelm

A common hiccup for wanna be entrepreneurs is envisioning a giant business, and then feeling overwhelmed by the thought of creating a large and complex business, and therefore quitting before they have even begun. Your awesome business idea may grow to eventually be a huge corporation, but you don't need to start that way. Start with a small but manageable business and grow and expand as the business naturally grows and expands.

For example, an upscale doggy day care business can begin with a few dog-walking or dog-sitting clients. Walking a few dogs for money is a business! It's not a huge business, but you are exchanging your services for a fee. Hence you have a business. As customers come to appreciate the attention you show their dogs, and they begin to tell their friends, your business will grow. You don't need to begin day one with 100 clients.

All of the ideas we have talked about so far are similar in that you need to start somewhere and grow from there. If you want to be a novelist with a huge catalog of books, you have to start with the first one. If you want to be a major blogger, you still have to start with your first blog post. If you want to have a huge online store, you have to start with your first sale.

Dream big, but don't dream yourself out of starting. Begin with what you can do, with the time and money you currently posses. The saying "go big or go home" sounds great, but if you go big from day one, you may find yourself burned out, broke, and going home sooner than you thought! Challenge yourself, but be reasonable about what you can fit into your life. I am a firm believer that slow and steady will help you reach your goals with your sanity and relationships still intact!

Conclusion

My hope is that this book opened your eyes to new possibilities for creating a thriving small business. Don't tie yourself down to a business that isn't right for you by settling for the first business idea that pops in your head. By carefully considering all of your options throughout this book, you can choose the right small business for you from the beginning, leading to a rewarding journey with your own business.

I do believe in the countless rewards of creating and owning a small business. As a business owner, you learn to stretch yourself in new ways. Owning a business requires being on a constant journey for knowledge in new areas. Stretching your creative muscles is another huge benefit of business ownership. The confidence you gain by building something of your own and watching it succeed is immeasurable. There is also the more tangible aspect of business ownership that allows you to earn money in a way that brings you joy and happiness. You are no longer working just for a paycheck, but that part is nice too!

Creating a small business can be perfect for people in many stages of life. Whether you have a full-time job you want to keep, have a full-time job you want to leave, are a stay-at-home parent, or a retired professional, by tailoring your business to you, you can start a business that fits in with your life and goals.

Be choosy about the topic of your business. Carefully

consider your personality and dreams as you wade through the types of business, and, finally, craft that perfect business idea.

For help getting started with your business, head to my website Small Business Sarah[38]. I am your small business tax and accounting tour guide! The tax and accounting side of running a business can feel overwhelming, but my goal is to make that part of running your business easy and painless. By signing up for my newsletter[39] you will receive my Small Business Startup Checklist to walk you through all the initial steps of creating a business.

Last but not least, browse through my Pinterest boards, each centered on a different type of businesses. From general business ideas, such as blogging or service-based businesses, to specific boards for gardening businesses, cooking businesses, and photography businesses, I have covered a wide range of clever and interesting small business ideas. You can find me on Pinterest at Small Biz Sarah[40]. Each board has numerous articles that will help you dive into the specifics of your chosen type of business and will provide you with a great start.

Here's to your small business success!

-Sarah

More from Sarah Korhnak

You've taken the big leap of starting your own business, don't be overwhelmed with worry about registering your business or about your business taxes. Quickly and easily understand your small business taxes with one of my tax guide books.

For Bloggers and other online business owners, The Blogger's Simple Guide to Taxes[41].

For Etsy Sellers and Product Sellers, The Etsy Seller's Simple Guide to Taxes[42].

For Virtual Assistant's (VA's) and other self-employed individuals, The VA's Guide to Taxes[43].

Notes

Introduction

[1] www.SmallBusinessSarah.com
[2] Sign up for my newsletter at www.SmallBusinessSarah.com/newsletter
[3] www.Pinterest.com/SmallBizSarah

Product Sales

[4] www.GatheredandSown.Etsy.com
[5] www.TheAmateurNaturalist.Etsy.com
[6] For Etsy seller advice check out www.MakerySpace.com
[7] https://Woocommerce.com/
[8] www.Shopify.com
[9] www.BigCommerce.com
[10] www.BigCartel.com
[11] www.Wix.com

[12] www.Cratejoy.com
[13] www.SmartPassiveIncome.com

Service-Based Business

[14] www.Fiverr.com

Writing

[15] www.BuildingAFramework.com
[16] www.CreateSpace.com
[17] www.ACX.com
[18] www.Authority.pub

[19] www.TheWriteLife.com

[20] www.ElnaCain.com

Speaking

[21] www.Toastmasters.org

[22] http://www.smartpassiveincome.com/tutorials/start-podcast-pats-complete-step-step-podcasting-tutorial/

Teaching

[23] www.GatheredAndSown.Etsy.com

[24] www.Skype.com

[25] www.Teachable.com

[26] www.Udemy.com

[27] www.Skillshare.com

[28] www.Clarity.fm

Video

[29] https://www.youtube.com/yt/press/statistics.html

[30] www.YouTube.com

[31] www.Famebit.com

[32] www.VidProMom.com

Business Essentials

[33] www.MailChimp.com

[34] www.AWeber.com

[35] www.ConvertKit.com

[36] www.MadMimi.com

[37] www.SocialMediaExaminer.com

Conclusion

[38] www.SmallBusinessSarah.com

[39] Sign up for the Small Business Sarah newsletter at www.SmallBusinessSarah.com/newsletter

[40] www.Pinterest.com/SmallBizSarah

More from Sarah Korhnak

[41] The Blogger's Simple Guide to Taxes by Sarah Korhnak.
https://www.books2read.com/u/3LrlaM

[42] The Etsy Seller's Simple Guide to Taxes.
https://www.books2read.com/u/m2X7Do

[43] The VA's Guide to Taxes by Sarah Korhnak
books2read.com/u/mqpXjZ